D0768833

DOG TRICKS

Teaching Your Doggie to Shake Hands and Other Tricks

By Liz Palika

CAPSTONE PRESS
a capstone imprint

Edge Books are published by Capstone Press,
1710 Roe Crest Drive, North Mankato, Minnesota 56003.
www.capstonepub.com

Library of Congress Cataloging-in-Publication Data
Palika, Liz, 1954-
  Dog tricks : teaching your doggie to shake hands and other tricks / by Liz Palika.
    p. cm. — (Edge books. Dog ownership)
  Includes bibliographical references and index.
  Summary: "Describes step-by-step instructions to teach a dog tricks"—Provided
by publisher.
  ISBN 978-1-4296-6526-1 (library binding)
  1. Dogs—Training—Juvenile literature. I. Title.
  SF431.P3365 2012
  636.7'0835—dc22   2011003789

Editorial Credits
Angie Kaelberer, editor; Bobbie Nuytten and Ashlee Suker, designers;
    Marcie Spence, media researcher; Eric Manske, production specialist

Photo Credits
Capstone Studio: Karon Dubke, 4, 6, 7, 8, 9, 11, 12, 13, 14, 17, 19, 20, 21,
22, 25, 26,; iStockphoto: tderden, cover; photolibrary/Peter Arnold/J-L. Klein
& M-L. Hubert, 29; Shutterstock: Dee Hunter, 1 (bottom), Dolly, 1 (top),
Eky Studio, 5, HASLOO, design element, hd connelly, design element, Lisa
Fischer, design element, stocksock, design element, tstockphoto, 28, Vitaly
Titov & Maria Sidelnikova, 15

Printed in the United States of America in Stevens Point, Wisconsin.
122011   006527WZVMI

Table of Contents

TRICKS

TRAINING TIP

Some dogs respond better to toys than to treats during trick training. You can try both to see which your dog prefers.

Before You Begin

Teaching your dog to perform tricks is a great way to enjoy time with your dog. Dogs naturally want to please their owners, so learning tricks can be fun for both of you.

You will need a few things before you begin to teach your dog tricks. For some tricks, you'll have a leash hooked to your dog's collar. The leash will keep your dog close to you as you teach her.

Tasty treats make training easier. Small pieces of cooked chicken, bits of hot dog, or store-bought dog treats all work well. Ask an adult to help you choose a good treat. An adult can also help you decide how many treats your dog should get each day so she doesn't become overweight. Eventually your dog will learn the command or signal and won't need the treat to perform the trick.

For some difficult tricks, give your dog a "jackpot" or a small handful of treats. A jackpot of treats tells your dog she has done a really good job and you're happy with her.

Once you begin teaching your dog, try to practice every day. Daily training sessions will help your dog learn and will make you a better dog trainer.

Shake Hands

Have you ever been offered a hand to shake when you meet a new person? Your dog can learn to do the same thing.

Step 1: Have your dog sit. If your dog has a leash on, drop it to the ground and step on it. This will keep her from moving away. Have one treat in your left hand and several more in your pocket.

Step 2: There's a little indentation below each of your dog's ankles at the back of her front legs. Using one finger of your right hand, tickle her right front leg in this place.

Step 3: When she lifts her paw away from your finger, even just a little, praise her using her name. For example, if your dog were named Pepper, you'd tell her, "Pepper, shake, good shake!" Give her a treat. Practice five times and take a break to play with her.

Step 4: After some practice, your dog may begin to lift her paw when you reach toward her. When she does, place your right hand under her paw as if you were shaking hands. Praise her and give her a treat.

indentation—a shallow spot

TRAINING TIP

Your dog should know its name and some basic commands like come, sit, and lie down before you start trick training.

As she gets better at lifting up her paw, hold out your hand and encourage her to put it in your hand by saying, "Shake!" Hold your hand just a tiny bit higher at each practice session. You want your dog to lift her paw to your hand rather than you lowering your hand to her paw.

High Five

Athletes often reach high and slap a teammate's hand after a good play. A high five says, "Good work!"

When your dog is doing the shake very well, teach her the high five. Begin with the word "shake" because she already knows that means to reach her paw toward your hand.

Step 1: Have a treat in your left hand and more in your pocket.

Step 2: Tell your dog, "Pepper, shake high five!" Place your open right hand in front of her. Your palm should be facing toward her and your fingers should be pointed up.

Step 3: When she reaches her paw toward you, touch her paw with your hand and praise her, "Pepper, good high five!" Give her a treat. Practice five times and then play with her.

After a couple of training sessions, stop saying "shake" and just tell her, "Pepper, high five!" With practice, your dog should learn to reach up to touch your hand instead of you touching hers.

Crawl

Have you ever wanted a snake as a pet? You can teach your dog to crawl on her belly, just like a snake does!

For this trick you will need a coffee table or other low table. You can also use a picnic table bench. It should be low enough so that your dog has to crawl under it. If you have a very small dog, you can use a step stool or footstool.

Step 1: Have some treats in your pocket and one in your hand.

Step 2: Ask your dog to sit on one side of the bench or table. Let her sniff the treat. Hold the treat in the air as you move it from her nose down to her paws. As you do this, tell her, "Pepper, lie down." When she does, praise her but don't yet give her the treat.

Step 3: Move to the other side of the bench. Reach under the bench with the treat so your dog sees it. Tell her, "Pepper, crawl!" Use the treat to guide her under the bench and to you. Praise her, "Good crawl!" and give her the treat. Practice five times and then take a play break.

9

The Weave

This trick is easy to teach but looks difficult. When people see you and your dog do this, they will be amazed.

Step 1: Drop your dog's leash to the ground. Have a treat in your right hand. Stand with your legs far enough apart for your dog to walk between them.

Step 2: Let your dog sniff the treat in your right hand. Move your right hand behind your right leg, letting your dog see the treat between your legs. Encourage her to move toward the treat.

Step 3: As she moves toward the treat, say, "Pepper, weave!" Lead her with the treat so she walks between your legs. She should then walk in a circle around your right leg back to the front. Give her the treat and praise her. Practice five times and then play with her.

weave—to move from side to side or in and out

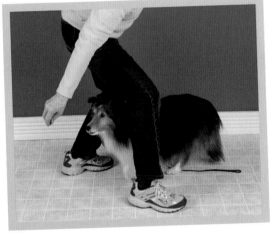

Step 4: When your dog will walk between your legs and circle around your right leg without stopping, add the second part of the trick. Hold a treat in your left hand. After she circles your right leg, use the treat to bring her between your legs again and then circle your left leg. You are having her make a figure eight shape around both of your legs. When she comes back to the front, praise her and give her the treat. Practice five times before taking a break.

Roll Over

Rolling over is a trick many dogs do on their own. Once your dog learns to roll over on command, you can teach her to roll in the opposite direction.

Step 1: Have one treat in your right hand and several treats in your pocket. Ask your dog to lie down. Gently roll her onto her side.

Step 2: Let your dog sniff the treat in your right hand. Hold the treat close to her nose. In a circular motion, bring the treat over her back.

Step 3: Keep moving the treat over her back. She should roll from her side onto her back to follow the treat. As she begins rolling, tell her, "Pepper, roll over! Good girl!" Keep moving the treat away from her so she rolls all the way over.

If your dog tries to get up to get the treat, keep your left hand on her shoulder or side to keep her in the down position.

Roll Back

Roll back teaches your dog to roll the other direction. Use the training steps from "roll over," except reverse the direction with the treat when you tell her, "Roll back."

Go to Sleep

Once your dog learns this trick, you can use a pillow and a blanket to make it look real.

Step 1: Have a treat in one hand and a few more in your pocket. Ask your dog to lie down.

Step 2: Sit or kneel next to your dog. Pull her over onto her side. As you do this, tell her, "Pepper, go to sleep."

Step 3: Let your dog sniff the treat in your hand. Then move the hand to the ground so she puts her head on the ground. Give her the treat and praise her. Practice five times before taking a break and playing with her.

Step 4: When your dog will do this trick and remain still for a few seconds, place a pillow under her head. Then lightly place a blanket over her. Praise her, "Pepper, good girl to go to sleep!"

Spin

When you were younger, you probably enjoyed spinning around in a circle. This also can be fun for your dog.

Step 1: Hold a treat in your right hand.

Step 2: With your dog standing in front of you, let her sniff the treat. Tell her, "Pepper, spin right," as you move the treat from her nose toward your right, which is her left. Move slowly so her nose follows the treat.

TRAINING TIP

Don't ask your dog to spin more than three or four times in a row. Your dog may get dizzy and sick.

Step 3: As your dog's nose follows the treat, move it toward her tail and then to your left. Make a big circle that ends in front of you.

Step 4: As your dog turns in a circle to follow the treat, praise her by saying, "Pepper, good spin right!" When she's again facing you, give her the treat and praise her some more. Practice five times and then take a break. When your dog is moving in a circle quickly, begin making your hand signal circle smaller.

Take a Bow!

Musicians and actors bow to their audience to thank them for their attention and applause. Your dog may not have an audience of fans, but she can learn to bow as well.

Step 1: Have your dog stand sideways in front of you, facing to your right. Have a treat in your right hand.

Step 2: Let her sniff the treat in your right hand. Tell her, "Pepper, bow," as you lower the treat from her nose to the ground right between her front paws. At the same time, put your left hand under her stomach to keep her hips raised. Her hips should stay up while her front end lies down.

Step 3: When her front end is down and her hips are still up, praise her, "Pepper, good bow!" and give her the treat. Practice five times and then play with your dog for a few minutes. When your dog learns not to lie down, you can stop putting your hand under her stomach.

Jump

Start this trick with a plastic hula hoop. When your dog understands the trick, you can ask her to jump over all kinds of things.

Step 1: Have a treat in one hand and the hoop in the other. Or you can ask another person to hold the hoop. Hold the hoop upright so your dog can jump through it.

Step 2: Rest the bottom of the hoop on the ground in front of your dog. Hold the treat in front of your dog's nose and let her sniff it.

Step 3: Use the treat to lead your dog through the hoop. As she follows the treat through the hoop, praise her, "Pepper, jump! Good!" and give her the treat. Do this five times and then let her rest for a couple of minutes.

After the break, repeat steps 1 through 3, but hold the edge of the hoop a couple of inches off the ground. After several training sessions, you can lift it a few inches higher.

TRAINING TIP

Measure your dog from the ground to the shoulders to figure out how high she can jump. Dogs can jump about 2 inches (5 centimeters) below the height of their shoulders.

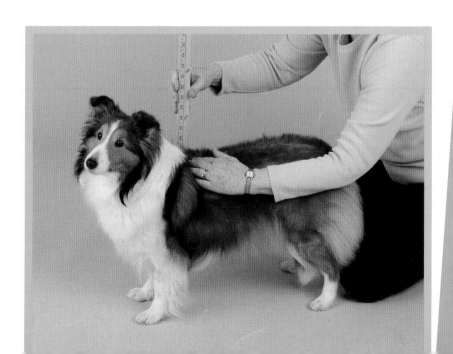

Teach your Dog to Read

You really can't teach your dog to read, but you can teach your dog to recognize the letters A, B, and C. People will be amazed at how smart your dog is!

At a craft store, buy three cutout letters. They should be about 2 inches (5 centimeters) tall. You can use A, B, and C.

Step 1: Begin with the letter "A."

Step 2: Hold the letter in front of your dog. With the other hand, hold a treat behind the letter. When your dog sniffs for the treat and touches the letter, say, "Pepper, A! Good A!" Then give her the treat.

Practice 10 times and take a break. Then repeat step 2. When your dog moves her nose toward the letter on her own, praise her and give her the treat.

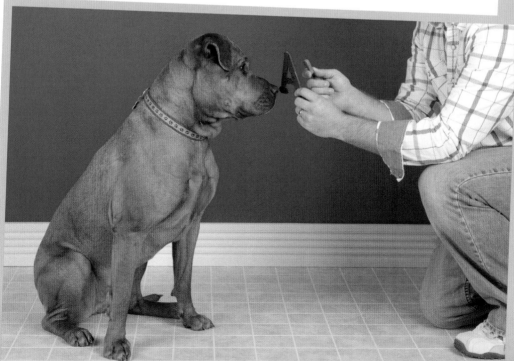

Step 3: Begin offering the letter without placing the treat behind it. Tell your dog, "Pepper, A." Praise her and give her a treat when she touches the letter.

When your dog will do steps 1 through 3 well with the first letter, put the first letter away. Bring out the letter "B." Repeat steps 1 through 3, teaching your dog to recognize the letter "B" just as you did for "A." Then do the same thing for the third letter.

Step 4: Now comes the hard part. Bring out all three letters. Have a bowl of treats close to you but out of your dog's reach.

Show your dog two of the letters and ask her to touch one on command. If she does, praise her, "Pepper, awesome to touch A! Good!" and give her a treat. Do this several times, alternating the letters. Then take a break and praise your dog. When you train again, alternate between the first and second letters. Once she can recognize both of them consistently, add the third letter to the mix.

If your dog touches the wrong letter, don't say or do anything. Just wait. If she continues to touch the wrong one, put that one on the table and hold up the correct one. Praise her when she touches it. Then pick up the other one and try again.

alternate—to take turns

Wait for It

Everyone will be amazed at your dog's self-control when she sits motionless as you place a dog biscuit on each front paw. While learning this trick, your dog isn't allowed to eat the dog biscuits. Give her the normal training treats as a reward instead.

Step 1: Have some of your dog's training treats in your pocket. Have your dog's leash in one hand and two dog biscuits in the other hand.

Step 2: Ask your dog to sit. Hold your dog's leash as you kneel or stand in front of her. Tell her, "Pepper, wait for it!" and place a dog biscuit on the ground in front of each of her front paws. If she moves her head toward the biscuits, use your hand on the leash to stop her. Tell her again, "Pepper, wait for it."

Step 3: After a few seconds, quickly pick up the biscuits. Put them in your pocket. Praise her, "Pepper, good to wait for it!" and give her several treats. Practice five times, praise her, and take a break.

Step 4: Do a couple of training sessions each day. Over time, your dog will learn to hold still and not go for the biscuits. Once she can do that, follow steps 1 through 3 but place the biscuits on the ground so they are touching her paws.

Step 5: When your dog masters step 4, place the biscuits on top of her paws. When she obeys, praise her and give her a jackpot of treats.

Yes, Please

You can teach your dog to answer "yes" to a question by nodding her head. Ask your dog if she wants a treat and then give her a hand signal. People who see her

nod her head will think she's answering you, "Yes, please!"

Step 1: Have one treat in your hand and a few more treats in your pocket. Stand in front of your dog.

Step 2: Let your dog sniff the treat in your hand. Then slowly move your hand a few inches higher than her nose so she looks up. Then move it a few inches lower so she looks down. Praise her and give her the treat. Practice 10 times and stop for a play session.

Step 3: After two training sessions, ask her to move her head up and down a couple of times before you praise her and give her the treat.

Step 4: After a few more training sessions, make your hand movement closer to your body rather than right in front of her nose. When she follows your hand signal there, praise her and give her a jackpot of treats.

No, Thank You

You can also teach your dog to politely say "no." To do this, use the same training steps that you used to teach your dog to say, "yes." But instead, make the hand signal from side to side. The command will be "No, thank you."

Quality Time

Teaching your dog tricks is a great way to bond with your dog. Just be sure to always make training fun by including lots of praise and following your training sessions with play. When a dog is having fun, she is much more willing to do what you ask of her. Let's shake on that!

Dogs that learn to follow their owners' commands are more likely to be well-behaved at home and out in public.

GLOSSARY

alternate (AWL-tur-nayte)—to take turns

audience (AW-dee-uhns)—people who watch or listen to a play, movie, or show

indentation (in-den-TAY-shuhn)—a shallow spot

jackpot (JAK-pot)—a large amount of something

session (SESH-uhn) – a period of time used for an activity

weave (WEEV)—to move from side to side or in and out

READ MORE

Eldredge, Kate, and Jacque Lynn Schultz.
Amazing Pet Tricks. ASPCA Kids. Hoboken, N.J.:
Wiley, 2009.

Nester, Mary Ann. *Smart Tricks for Smart Dogs: A
Fun and Easy Step-by-Step Program for Every Dog.*
Neptune City, N.J.: T.F.H. Publications, 2009.

Pang, Evelyn, and Hilary Louie. *Good Dog!
Kids Teach Kids about Dog Behavior and Training.*
Wenatchee, Wash.: Dogwise Pub., 2008.

Pavia, Audrey, and Jacque Lynn Schultz. *Having
Fun with your Dog.* ASPCA Kids. Hoboken, N.J.:
Wiley, 2009.

INTERNET SITES

FactHound offers a safe, fun way to find Internet
sites related to this book. All of the sites on
FactHound have been researched by our staff.

Here's all you do:

Visit *www.facthound.com*

Type in this code: 9781429665261

Check out projects, games and lots more at
www.capstonekids.com

INDEX